Science Experiments

ELECTRICITY

by
John Farndon

Benchmark Books

MARSHALL CAVENDISH

NEW YORK

Marshall Cavendish Corporation

99 White Plains Road

Tarrytown, New York 10591-9001

© 2001 Marshall Cavendish Corporation

Created by Brown Partworks Ltd

Library of Congress Cataloging-in-Publication Data

Farndon, John

    Electricity / by John Farndon
    p. cm. — (Science experiments)
    Includes index.
    ISBN 0-7614-1086-4 (lib. bdg.)
    1. Electricity—Experiments—Juvenile literature. [1. Electricity—
Experiments. 2. Experiments.] I. Title.

QC527.2 .F37 2001   00-039752
537'.078—dc21

Printed in Hong Kong

PHOTOGRAPHIC CREDITS

t – top; b – bottom; c – center; l – left; r – right

Corbis - title page, Paul A Souders (c); p4,5 Richard Hamilton Smith (b);
p5 (br); p8,9 Roger Ressmeyer (b); p12,13 Paul A Souders (b); p19 (br);
p22 Craig Aurness (b); p24,25 Roger Ressmeyer (b); p25 Randy Faris (tr);
p28,29 Steve Chenn (b)
The Image Bank - p18 Tom Mareschal (bl)
Leslie Garland - p23 Andrew Lambert (cr)
Pictor - p29 (br)

Step-by-step photography throughout: Martin Norris

Front cover: Martin Norris

Contents

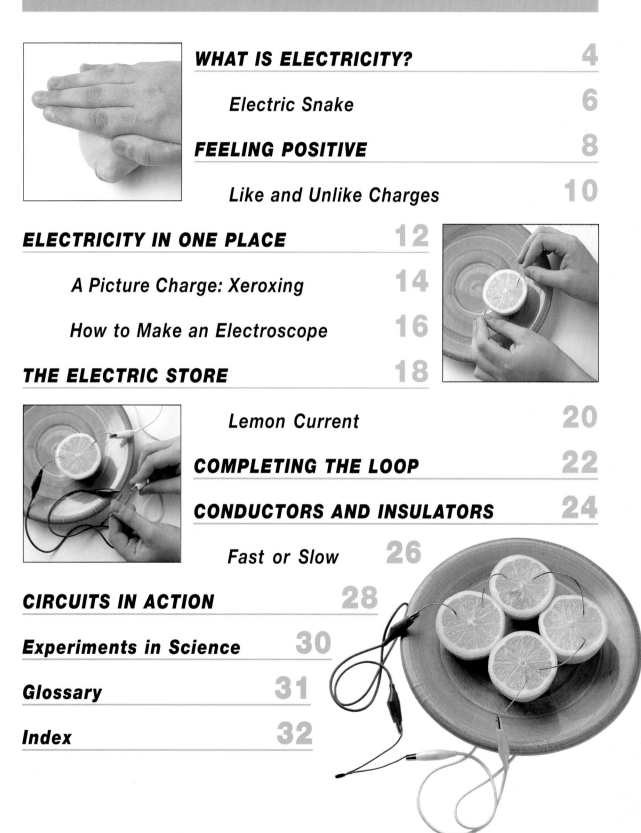

WHAT IS ELECTRICITY?

Electricity is an amazing force. It can make lights shine and bring water to a boil. It can make the music on a CD player and create the picture in a TV tube. It can power anything from the thousands of tiny microswitches in a computer to the huge engines in a train. In fact electricity is one of the basic forces that holds every single atom in the universe together.

Electricity has been around for a very, very long time. It was formed in the first split second of the universe, more than 12 billion years ago. Yet electricity was barely noticed until little more than 200 years ago.

Did you know?

WHY IS IT CALLED ELECTRICITY?

The word "electricity" comes from the Ancient Greeks. In about 600 B.C., Greek philosopher Thales noticed that when he rubbed a kind of resin called amber with cloth, the amber attracted feathers, threads, and bits of fluff. The Greek word for amber was *elektron*. The word "electricity" was coined by William Gilbert, Queen Elizabeth I's physician (doctor). He was conducting some experiments, and he noticed that sulfur had the same power of attraction as amber when rubbed. He called this force of attraction electricity.

Big cities use huge amounts of electricity for power.

People had seen lightning flashing through the sky, but no-one realized that the lightning was electric. The Ancient Greeks noticed minor effects on a few tiny stones.

Important discoveries about electricity were made in the 1820s and 1830s by men such as Michael Faraday and Joseph Henry. Faraday and Henry found that electricity was closely linked to magnetism. They discovered that electricity could move magnets to make electric motors. More importantly, they found that moving magnets could generate electricity.

Once people knew how to generate electricity at will, the way was open to the modern world of electrical technology, which brought us everything from electric lights to fast and powerful computers.

By the mid-18th century, scientists had built machines that created a powerful surge of electricity by rubbing glass and sulfur together. They stored electricity in a special kind of glass jar, called a Leyden jar. The electricity could be drawn from the jar by means of a brass chain. Some scientists got nasty shocks this way!

In the real world

In 1752, American statesman and scientist Benjamin Franklin showed that lightning was electric. He flew a kite in a thunderstorm, and electricity flowed down the string as lightning flashed.

Franklin was extremely lucky to survive his experiment with electricity. Many scientists who repeated it were electrocuted. But Franklin's test kindled enormous interest in electricity, and soon scientists were discovering all kinds of things about it.

This painting by Benjamin West is called "Benjamin Franklin Drawing Electricity From the Sky." It shows Franklin's famous experiment.

ELECTRIC SNAKE

You will need

- ✔ metal plate or cookie tin lid
- ✔ nylon or silk scarf
- ✔ plastic pen
- ✔ tissue paper
- ✔ scissors

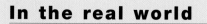

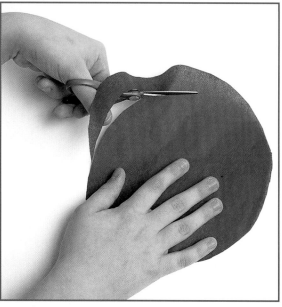

1 Cut out a disk of tissue paper 8 in (20 cm) in diameter. Use the scissors to cut the disk into a spiral about ¾ in (2 cm) wide.

In the real world

Have you ever gotten an electric shock while you are shopping? If you walk over a nylon carpet in a warm, dry atmosphere, your body can build up an electric charge. When you touch something metal, such as a clothes rack, a spark leaps from your body to the metal. You can try this at home by taking your shoes off and rubbing your bare feet on the carpet, then reaching for a door handle or metal furniture such as a filing cabinet. The electricity will leap from your body when your hand is very close to the metal object.

2 Lay the tissue on top of the plate or lid. Then rub the plastic pen vigorously with the scarf.

In focus

You can see the power of electricity by rubbing a balloon on a wool sweater. Hold the balloon against your sweater, and you can let go—it will stick in place. You can do the same by rubbing the balloon on your hair. If you lift the balloon up (like the snake spiral), you will get some hair-raising results!

If you rub a balloon against a wool vest, it will stick to your body when you let go.

What is happening?

All these effects are caused by what is called static electricity. When certain substances rub together, an electrical force called a "charge" is created between them that either attracts or repels. What happens is that minute pieces called electrons get knocked off the atoms in one substance and stick to the atoms in the other.

Substances that lose electrons are said to be positively charged; those that gain them are said to be negatively charged. Unlike charges attract each other; like charges repel.

Hold the pen over the center of the spiral snake and lift the pen slowly: the tissue will spiral upward.

FEELING POSITIVE

Queen Elizabeth I's physician William Gilbert showed that several substances possessed "electricity"—the power of attraction. In 1733, French chemist Charles Dufay discovered that the same substances also had the power of repulsion. Amber rubbed with a cloth attracts fluff and threads, but it pushes away another piece of rubbed amber. Rubbed glass will attract amber but push away fluff.

Dufay explained all this by suggesting that electricity must be two different kinds of "fluid." Put unlike kinds together and they attract each other; put like kinds together and they repel.

A balloon that has been rubbed against a cat's fur will become negatively charged. If the balloon is held near the cat, it will attract the cat's fur.

In the real world

Your clothes sometimes feel hard when they come out of the wash. This is because the fibers in certain fabrics, especially synthetics, rub together in the wash and exchange electrons. An electrical charge builds up on the fabric, making the fibers cling together so that they feel slightly stiff. Fabric conditioners in the wash lubricate the fibers and reduce the buildup of electrical charge. The fibers slide more easily over each other, and the fabric feels softer.

American statesman and scientist Benjamin Franklin thought electricity was a kind of fluid, too. But he thought there was just one fluid. When glass is rubbed, he thought, electrical fluid flows into it, making it "positively charged." "Charged" is another word for "filled." When amber is rubbed, he thought, electrical fluid flows out of it, making it "negatively charged." Whenever glass and amber come into contact, Franklin thought that fluid would flow from positive to negative until the fluids were equally balanced.

We now know that Franklin was not so far from the truth, except that it is tiny particles called electrons that are involved, not fluids (see the box). The electricity balances, or discharges, by flowing from the amber to the glass, not the other way around. When amber is rubbed with cloth, or when you rub a balloon on a sweater, electrons from the cloth rub off onto the amber or from the sweater onto the balloon. The electrons are negatively charged, so the rubbed amber and the balloon become negatively charged. The cloth and the sweater lose electrons, so they become positively charged. The difference in charge draws them together.

In focus

Everything in the universe is made up of tiny bits called atoms. Atoms are so small that two billion could fit on the period at the end of this sentence. Inside every atom there are particles called electrons. Electrons are millions of times smaller than atoms. Atoms are mostly empty space, with just a tiny core, or nucleus, in the center. The nucleus is a tight cluster of two kinds of particles called protons and neutrons. Electrons whizz around the nucleus in a series of rings. Electrons have a "negative" electrical charge and attract protons. Protons have a "positive" electrical charge and attract electrons.

Neutrons have no charge. Normally, electrons are held closely to the atom by their attraction to the protons. But some outer electrons are held loosely and occasionally come away from the atom altogether. It is these loose electrons that cause the effects we know as electricity.

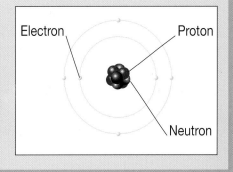

LIKE AND UNLIKE CHARGES

You will need

✔ roll of plastic electrical tape

✔ plastic mug

✔ scissors

1 Use the scissors to cut off a length of tape about 6 in (15 cm) long and stick the end of it to a plastic mug.

Now try this

Blow up a balloon and tie the end to hold the air in. Turn the cold faucet on in a large sink or bath tub to create a stream about ⅛ in (3 mm) across. When you move the balloon close to—but not touching—the water, nothing will happen. However, if you rub the balloon on your sweater several times and hold it close to the water, the water will bend toward the balloon. Rubbing the balloon makes it gain electrons from your sweater, so it becomes negatively charged. The negatively charged balloon draws the uncharged water toward it.

Holding the balloon close to the water will make the water bend toward the balloon.

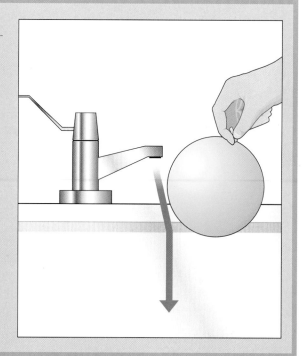

2 Cut off another 6-in (15-cm) length. Move it toward the first piece. Both pieces curl away—they repel each other.

3 Lightly stroke one piece of tape between your finger and thumb several times.

What is happening?

As each piece of tape is pulled off the roll, it pulls some electrons with it. The electrons give the tape a negative charge of electricity. Both pieces of tape have the same negative charge so they repel each other. Stroking the tape neutralizes its charge so that the unstroked, charged piece of tape is drawn toward it. A charged object is always drawn toward an uncharged object because there is a difference in charge.

Now try moving the two pieces of tape together. This time they jump toward each other. They are attracted.

ELECTRICITY IN ONE PLACE

Whenever two materials are rubbed together, tiny electrons can jump from one to the other and so create a charge of static electricity. Charges like these are being created in the world all the time. Every time you comb your hair, for instance, you are making static electricity.

Most charges are too small for you to notice anything. But static charges can also create one of the most spectacular events in nature—lightning.

Lightning is created in the same way as all static electricity: by the transfer of electrons between atoms. Thunderclouds are gigantic, and air currents tear up and down violently inside them. As they do, they sweep billions of tiny ice crystals and water droplets past each other. The crystals and droplets collide with each other and transfer electrons. The crystals take on a negative charge, and

When the girl touches the generator, all her hairs become charged, and each one repels the others.

In the real world

In the 1930s, American physicist Robert Van de Graaff invented a device now called the Van de Graaff generator. This generator creates a gigantic static charge, which is built up by rollers on a belt of special fabric. The belt carries the charge into a big metal ball where it can create spectacular effects. Small tabletop Van de Graaff generators sometimes used in schools can generate anything from 5,000 to half a million volts. When you touch them, your hair stands on end because the charge in each hair repels the charges in the other hairs. Big generators several stories high can produce many millions of volts.

the droplets become positively charged. As the cloud builds up, the negatively charged ice crystals sink to the bottom, while the positively charged water droplets rise to the top.

Soon a huge charge difference builds up in the cloud. The base of the cloud becomes negatively charged, while the top of the cloud takes a positive charge.

Lightning flashes as the extra electrons in the base of the cloud shoot down to the ground (fork lightning) or up to the

positive cloud top (sheet lightning). This electrical discharge can be hundreds of millions of volts strong.

Obviously lightning can be dangerous. But even small static charges can cause problems. Humans cannot detect a static charge of less than 2,500 volts. When you feel a tingle as you touch a metal light switch, the current is 3,000 volts or more. Sliding across a long carpet in a centrally heated building, you can generate up to 30,000 volts.

Many computer components are designed to run at just 5 volts. So even a 10-volt static discharge could easily burn them out. This is why engineers working with electronic parts take great care to reduce static: using antistatic sprays, wearing antistatic bracelets, keeping the air moist, and so on.

A PICTURE CHARGE: XEROXING

You will need

✔ sheet of dark plastic (such as a plastic folder)

✔ old dish towel or cloth

✔ talcum powder

✔ electrical tape

1 In a place where it is safe to spill talcum powder, stick two lengths of 6 in (15 cm) of tape onto the plastic sheet.

In focus

Xerox machines create images with black toner rather than talcum powder. Inside, a roller drum coated with a light-sensitive material called selenium is given an electrical charge. A light scans across the picture to be copied and beams it onto the drum via mirrors. Selenium conducts electricity better when exposed to light, so the electric charge flows away from the picture's lighter areas and stays on the dark areas. Then negatively charged toner powder is dusted onto the drum. It sticks to the positively charged, dark areas because opposite charges attract. The drum rolls over a sheet of paper, transferring the picture to the paper.

3 Hold the plastic sheet flat with one hand and carefully peel the tape away with the other hand.

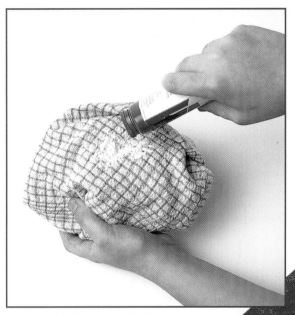

What is happening?

Peeling the tape off the plastic leaves a charged area behind. This charge attracts the powder, creating an image in powder where the tape has been peeled off.

2 Sprinkle some talcum powder onto the towel and rub it in.

4 Shake talcum powder from the towel as evenly as you can about 8 in (20 cm) above the plastic.

You will find that the powder is attracted to the area of plastic from which you peeled the tape.

HOW TO MAKE AN ELECTROSCOPE

You will need

- ✓ a piece of aluminum foil about ⅝ in (1.5 cm) wide and 2¼ in (6 cm) long
- ✓ another small piece of aluminum foil
- ✓ 4 in (10 cm) of stiff wire
- ✓ small piece of cardboard
- ✓ silk handkerchief
- ✓ plastic tape
- ✓ a small glass jar
- ✓ plastic comb
- ✓ scissors

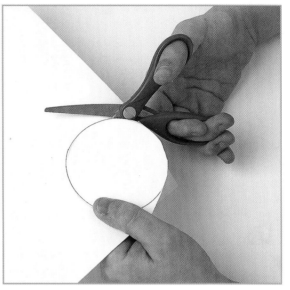

1 Draw around the top of the jar on the cardboard. Cut out the disk. It should fit the top of the jar exactly. Bend the last ¾ in (2 cm) of the wire into a right angle.

What is happening?

You have made a very simple electroscope, a device for indicating a static charge. When you hold a positively charged object, such as the comb, near the ball at the top, the positive charge draws negative charges up the wire into the ball. This drains the foil strip of negative charge, making it very slightly positive. Since both halves of the strip now have the same charge, they fly apart. The amount they fly apart depends on the strength of the charge on the object you are testing. You can use the electroscope to test other things, such as pieces of adhesive tape peeled off the roll, for an electrical charge.

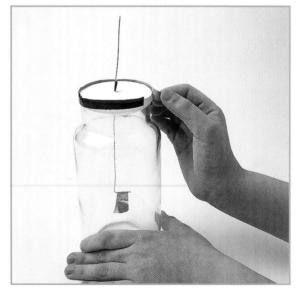

3 Gently lower the end of the wire with the foil strip into the jar until the cardboard sits on the rim of the jar. Tape the cardboard to the jar.

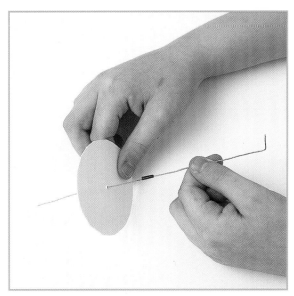

2 Push a third of the other end of the wire through the middle of the cardboard. Tape it in place. Fold the measured piece of foil. Tape it over the bent wire end.

4 Now crush the small piece of the aluminum foil into a ball about ¾ in (2 cm) across and push it onto the exposed end of the wire.

Rub a plastic comb vigorously on the silk to give it a static charge. Hold the comb close to the aluminum ball. Watch the ends of the foil strip fly apart.

THE ELECTRIC STORE

The battery in a flashlight has a single cell. It creates the electrical charge that lights the bulb.

Most of the static electrical charges described so far are created by two things rubbing together. But electrical charges can be created by chemical reactions as well. This is how batteries work.

Batteries come in all shapes and sizes. Some are as small as a pill or as thin as a sheet of paper. Others are as large as a refrigerator. All batteries create an electrical charge in the same way: two chemical substances

In the real world

The idea of chemically generated electricity was discovered by accident. In 1786, Italian anatomist Luigi Galvani had been experimenting with the legs of dead frogs. He managed to make them twitch with the electrical charge from a Leyden jar. Then he hung them on a railing in a thunderstorm to see if lightning would make them twitch. To his surprise, the legs twitched even before the storm arrived. Galvani believed he had discovered a new kind of electricity, made by the frog's nerves, and he called it "animal electricity."

Alessandro Volta suspected there was no such thing as animal electricity. In the 1790s, he found that the electricity was created by the chemical reaction between the metal of the railing and the metal hook on which the frog's legs hung.

react together, and electrons flow from one substance to the other. In an ordinary flashlight battery, for instance, these substances are zinc and carbon, while in an automobile battery, they are lead and lead dioxide.

The piece of the battery that creates the charge is called the cell. Some batteries, such as those in automobiles, are made from many cells. Most, such as flashlight batteries, are only a single cell.

Each cell has two electrodes, which are made of different substances. The electrodes are where the charge is concentrated. The negative electrode has more electrons; the positive electrode has fewer. Both electrodes are dipped in a special paste or liquid, which is called the electrolyte. Electrons migrate (move) from the positive battery terminal (end) to the negative terminal through the electrolyte.

The excess of electrons is in some ways like a bath full of water. If electrical wires are joined up in a loop to both electrodes, it is like opening the plughole. All at once, the pressure of all the extra electrons creates a flow of electricity right through the loop to the positive electrode. There is more information about "electrical currents" such as these on pages 22–23.

Did you know?

WHAT WOKE FRANKENSTEIN'S MONSTER?

When people first heard of Galvani's discovery of "animal electricity," they were very excited. Many believed that Galvani had stumbled on the secret to life itself. Animal electricity, they thought, was the amazing force that brought flesh and bone to life. Soon scientists across Europe were trying to bring corpses (dead bodies) back to life by electrifying them. They could make legs twitch, and even make eyes wink. The idea inspired Mary Shelley to write *Frankenstein* in 1819. In this famous story, a scientist named Dr. Frankenstein assembles pieces of human corpses to make a creature, which he brings to life with a massive electric shock from a bolt of lightning. This picture is from the film "Son of Frankenstein," which was made in 1939.

LEMON CURRENT

Before you begin

You will need to purchase a flashlight bulb and bulb holder from an electrical supply store.

You will need

- ✔ steel wire and copper wire
- ✔ wire cutters
- ✔ lemons
- ✔ knife

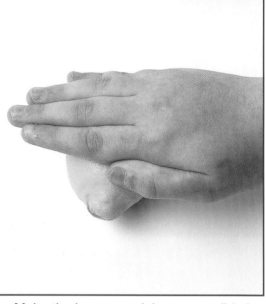

1 Make the lemons as juicy as possible by rolling them firmly on a table. Then cut one lemon in half.

What is happening?

The acidity of the lemon juice is making the metal in the two wires react. The chemical reaction strips the positive ions (atoms with electrons missing) from the steel and leaves it with an excess of negatively charged electrons. This sends an electrical current from the steel wire to the copper wire. The copper wire draws positive ions from the acid lemon juice and becomes positively charged. The bulb lights up as the current flows through it.

3 Now attach the other ends of the wires to the bulb holder. Does this make the bulb light up?

In the real world

Volta built the world's first battery, called a voltaic pile, in 1800. The pile was made with alternate layers of copper and zinc in a jar of salt water. The chemical reaction between the copper and zinc and the salt water created a steady supply of electricity.

2 Strip any plastic coating off the ends of the wires with the wire cutters. Push one end of each wire into opposite sides of one of the lemon halves.

If the bulb doesn't light, try connecting up more lemons in the same way, making sure each lemon half has one copper and one steel wire.

COMPLETING THE LOOP

Did you know?

The electrons inside an electric wire move slowly, only a few fractions of an inch per second. However, the overall effect of all these movements means that electrical energy is sent through a long circuit almost instantly. This is why a light comes on almost as soon as you flick the switch.

Lightning is a form of static electricity. Fork lightning occurs when negatively charged electrons in the base of a cloud shoot down to the ground.

Static electricity is so called because the charge stays in one place. Sometimes static electricity jumps from one place to another, but it is a single, brief jump. Static electrical charges can be enormous, such as lightning, but they are difficult to use as energy. All the electrical devices that we use today, from hairdryers to games consoles and computers, rely on continuously moving charges called "currents."

To create an electrical current, two things are needed. First, there must be an unbroken circuit for the current to flow through. The circuit is usually a loop of copper wire, since copper lets electrical charge pass through it. Second, there must be something to push the electrons that carry the charge through the circuit. This is called the electromotive force and is typically provided by a battery or a generator. A battery contains a cell or cells that create the electrical charge. Generators create the charge in a different way (see page 28).

In focus

Scientists once thought electricity flows through circuits like water, which is why it is called an electrical current. In fact, it is more like a row of marbles. If you flick the marble at one end, it cannons into the next, which bumps into the next, and so on down the row until the last one shoots off. The movement is passed down the row almost instantly.

The same is true in an electrical wire, only instead of marbles, it is "free" electrons that transmit the movement. These are electrons held so loosely to their atoms that they actually drift away into the space between atoms.

Free electrons in an electrical current act like a row of marbles, each one pushing the next along the circuit.

Normally, these free electrons wander at random throughout the material, but when an electrical current is switched on, they begin to move together. The electromotive force (a force that moves electrons) builds up a surplus of free electrons at one end of the circuit. Since like charges repel, these free electrons repel each other, pushing all the free electrons in the circuit away, just like the marbles. The current gets passed quickly through the circuit.

CONDUCTORS AND INSULATORS

Some materials transmit electricity very well. They are said to be good conductors. The best conductors are metals, which is why copper is used for wires. Metal atoms always have a few electrons that are only loosely held in place, so there are lots of free electrons to transmit the electric current.

Water also conducts electricity well, for the same reason. This is why it is very dangerous to go near electrical equipment with

High-voltage power lines are very good conductors of electricity.

In the real world

SUPERCONDUCTORS

Whenever electricity passes through a wire, a lot of its energy is lost on the way because of the wire's natural resistance. Even good conductors offer considerable resistance and so waste some electrical energy. But at very, very low temperatures, the resistance of certain special materials, called superconductors, almost vanishes. They transmit huge electric currents with very little energy loss. At the moment, super-conductivity occurs only at temperatures far too low to be practical. In future, scientists hope to make it occur at only a little below freezing (32°F, or 0°C), so superconducting electric motors could be used to power machines such as trains with very little energy.

wet hands. If your hands are wet, the water can seep into the switch and make instant contact with the electrical circuit inside, giving you a nasty shock.

Other materials do not conduct electricity because their electrons are not free to move. These materials are called insulators. Air, plastic, and rubber are good insulators. Electrical cables are coated in plastic because it is an insulator and so it stops the electricity escaping from the wires.

HOW ELECTRIC LIGHT BULBS WORK

Inside every light bulb there is a very thin piece of wire called the filament. This is part of the electrical circuit, but because it is so thin, it severely restricts the flow of electricity. Like a football crowd trying to push through a narrow turnstile, the atoms and electrons get squashed together. As they jostle together, they make the filament very hot—so hot that it glows. The glowing filament makes the light shine.

Why doesn't the filament burn out? Filaments are usually made of the tough metal tungsten, and they are held inside a glass bulb filled with a special nonreactive gas called argon. Burning is a chemical reaction that usually needs the oxygen in the air. Argon is nonreactive, so it will not allow burning. The filament does not last forever, though. Eventually it becomes so thin that it breaks, and the light bulb has to be replaced.

FAST OR SLOW

Before you begin

You will need to get a bulb holder and wires with clips attached from an electrical supply store. The battery should have metal flanges, for attaching the clips to. Make sure you buy suitable small wires and clips for the type of battery and bulb holder you are using.

You will need

✔ materials to test for resistance such as an eraser, a wooden ruler, a metal ruler, a plastic ruler, a lead pencil, scissors

✔ three wires with metal clips on the end

✔ flashlight bulb in a bulb holder

✔ battery

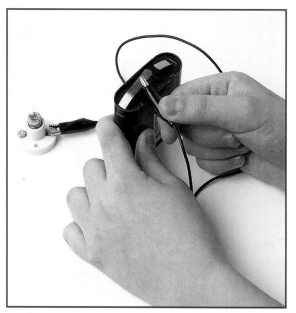

1 Connect one end of the first wire to the battery and the other end to one of the bulb flanges.

Now try this

Soak an ordinary wooden lead pencil in water overnight. Ask an adult to split the pencil in half lengthways, leaving the lead in one half of the pencil (they will have to use a scalpel or sharp craft knife to do this). Set up the circuit as in the experiment described here, then connect one free clip to the point of the pencil lead. Touch the second free clip on the lead some way along the pencil to complete the circuit and make the bulb light up.

Move the second clip backward and forward along the lead and watch the bulb growing brighter or dimmer: the shorter the circuit, the brighter the light will be.

2 Now connect one end of the second wire to the other bulb flange.

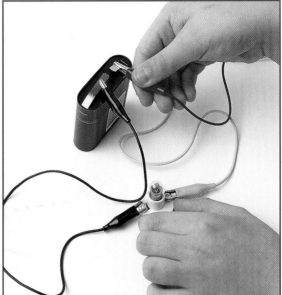

3 Connect one end of the third wire to the other battery terminal. You are left with two free clip ends.

What is happening?

RESISTANCE

When electrons bump into atoms in a conductor, the current is reduced. This is called resistance. Some materials, such as wood and rubber, offer a great deal of resistance. This diminishes the current and makes the light glow only dimly or even not at all. Also, the thinner and longer a conductor is, the greater the resistance it offers and the greater the loss of current.

See how brightly the bulb shines if you simply connect the two free clip ends. Now connect the free clips to each side of the material to be tested. The dimmer the bulb glows, the more resistant the material is.

CIRCUITS IN ACTION

There are many different kinds of electrical circuits. Some are minute, such as the tiny circuits etched onto the circuit boards inside a computer. Others are gigantic, such as the massive cables that carry electric power from power stations to your home. Large or small, all circuits have the same three elements.

First, there is a conductor through which the electricity flows. Second, there is a "load," which is the equipment the electricity is powering, such as a TV. Third, there is the energy source, which may be a battery or a generator. The energy is basically the difference in the number of electrons at the positive and negative terminals (ends) of the loop. This difference is called the "potential difference" and is measured in volts. The more energy a battery or generator

The voltage of the electricity supply is transformed to a lower level before it reaches homes. Computer circuits use only about 5 volts.

In the real world

AC/DC

Simple electricity generators are called dynamos. They work by spinning magnets inside a wire core. Dynamos give a current called direct current (DC), because it flows in only one direction. But generators in most cars and power stations are called alternators. They give an alternating current (AC) that swaps direction many times a second. This happens because as the magnets spin, they pass the wires going up on one side and down on the other. The advantage of AC over DC is that it can easily be transformed—its voltage can be stepped up or down. The voltage can be stepped up to transmit it large distances and down to make it safe to use.

gives, the bigger the voltage. Flashlights typically work with 1.5 or 3 volts. Electricity around the home is generally 120 volts or 240 volts, depending on which country you live in.

The rate (speed) at which the current flows is measured in amps. This depends on the voltage and the resistance the wire puts up. Resistance is measured in ohms, which are named after German scientist Georg Ohm (1789–1854) who discovered how voltage and current (amps) are related.

In focus

HOW ELECTRICITY GETS TO YOUR HOUSE

Electricity is generated in power stations by banks of huge alternators. It is then fed into a network of cables called the grid, which distributes it around the country. Power-station alternators push out 25,000 volts or so, which is far too much to use in the home yet not large enough to transmit long distances. So for transmission through the grid, the voltage is boosted to more than 400,000 volts by devices called step-up transformers. This high-voltage current is carried in special high-tension cables, either buried underground or suspended high up from tall towers called pylons. Near its destination, the voltage is reduced to 800 volts by step-down transformers at substations. From the substation it is distributed through underground cables called electricity mains to factories or further substations, where the voltage is cut again to a safe 110–240 volts for homes, shops, schools, and offices.

By the time electricity reaches your home, the voltage has been cut to a safe level.

Experiments in Science

Science is about knowledge: it is concerned with knowing and trying to understand the world around us. The word comes from the Latin word, *scire*, to know.

In the early 17th century, the great English thinker Francis Bacon suggested that the best way to learn about the world was not simply to think about it, but to go out and look for yourself—to make observations and try things out. Ever since then, scientists have tried to approach their work with a mixture of observation and experiment. Scientists insist that an idea or theory must be tested by observation and experiment before it is widely accepted.

All the experiments in this book have been tried before, and the theories behind them are widely accepted. But that it is no reason why you should accept them. Once you have done all the experiments in this book, you will know the ideas are true not because we have told you so, but because you have seen for yourself.

All too often in science there is an external factor interfering with the result which the scientist just has not thought of. Sometimes this can make the experiment seem to work when it has not, as well as making it fail. One scientist conducted lots of demonstrations to show that a clever horse called Hans could count things and tap out the answer with his hoof. The horse was indeed clever, but later it was found that rather than counting, he was getting clues from tiny unconscious movements of the scientist's eyebrows.

This is why it is very important when conducting experiments to be as rigorous as you possibly can. The more casual you are, the more "eyebrow factors" you will let in. There will always be some things that you can not control. But the more precise you are, the less these are likely to affect the outcome.

What went wrong?

However careful you are, your experiments may not work. If so, you should try to find out where you went wrong. Then repeat the experiment until you are absolutely sure you are doing everything right. Scientists learn as much, if not more, from experiments that go wrong as those that succeed. In 1929, Alexander Fleming discovered the first antibiotic drug, penicillin, when he noticed that a bacteria culture he was growing for an experiment had gone moldy—and that the mold seemed to kill the bacteria. A poor scientist would probably have thrown the moldy culture away. A good scientist is one who looks for alternative explanations for unexpected results.

Glossary

Alternating current (AC): A supply of electricity that constantly changes direction. It is the type of current that is supplied to homes and offices.

Amp: Unit of measurement of electrical energy.

Atoms: Every substance is made of invisibly tiny atoms, which are the smallest particle of any chemical element. Each atom has a nucleus, around which electrons whirl.

Battery: A source of electrical energy. A battery contains one or more cells.

Cell: Something that produces electrical energy from a chemical reaction.

Circuit: An unbroken path that electrical current flows around.

Conductor: A material that allows electricity to flow easily through it.

Current: The flow of electrical charge produced when electrons move.

Direct current (DC): A supply of electrical current that flows in just one direction. Batteries produce this type of electrical current.

Dynamo: A device that converts (changes) the energy of movement into electrical energy.

Electromotive force: A force that pushes electrons around a circuit.

Electron: A tiny particle that whizzes around the nucleus of an atom.

Filament: The very thin wire inside a light bulb that glows when electrical current flows through it. It is usually made of tungsten.

Fluid: A liquid or a gas. Early scientists thought that electricity was a fluid or a mixture of fluids.

Ion: An atom or group of atoms that have a positive or a negative charge.

Neutron: A minute particle found inside the nucleus of an atom. Neutrons are

neutral—they do not have an electrical charge.

Nucleus: The central part of an atom. It contains the protons and neutrons.

Ohm: Unit of measurement of electrical resistance.

Potential difference: The difference in the number of electrons in two parts of an electrical circuit.

Proton: A tiny particle with a positive charge. Protons are found inside the nucleus of an atom.

Resistance: The ability of a substance to resist the flow of electricity through it.

Superconductor: A substance that has hardly any electrical resistance.

Volt: Unit for measuring potential difference.

Index

A, B

alternating current 28, 31
antistatic devices 12, 13
atoms 4, 7, 27, 31
battery 18, 19, 21, 23, 28, 31

C, D

cell 19, 23, 31
chemical reaction 18, 20
circuit 23, 25, 26, 28, 31
computer 5, 13, 23, 28
conductor 24, 25, 28, 31
direct current 28, 31
Dufay, Charles 8
dynamo 28, 31

E, F

electrical charge 6, 7, 8, 9, 14. 16, 18
electrical current 19, 20, 23, 27, 31
electrodes 19
electrolyte 19
electromotive force 23, 31
electron 7, 8, 9, 10, 11, 12, 13, 19, 23, 27, 31
electroscope 16
fabric conditioner 8
Faraday, Michael 5
Franklin, Benjamin 5, 9

G, H, I

Galvani, Luigi 18, 19
generator 23, 28
Gilbert, William 4, 8
Henry, Joseph 5
insulator 24, 25, 31
ion 13, 20

L

Leyden jar 5, 18
light bulb 25, 26
lightning 5, 12, 13, 18, 19, 22

M

magnetism 5

N, O

neutron 9, 31
Ohm, George 29

P, Q

potential difference 28
proton 9

R

resistance 24, 27, 29, 31

S, T

Shelley, Mary 19
static electricity 7, 12, 13, 16, 17, 23
superconductor 24, 31
Thales 4

U

Van de Graaff, Robert 12
Van de Graaff generator 12
Volta, Alessandro 18, 21
voltaic pile 21

X

xerox machine 14